For Yoona, and all the other young curious minds.
Never stop dreaming.

Hayao Miyazaki

A Story of a Little Dreamer Who Captivated the World with Animation

Once upon a time, in Tokyo, Japan, there was a little boy named Hayao Miyazaki. His dad worked at a company that made airplane parts, so Hayao grew up watching airplanes and loved drawing them, too.

Hayao's mom was often very sick and spent a lot of time in the hospital. Despite this, she was bright, lively, and bravely fighting her illness.

These experiences filled Hayao with dreams of kind yet strong heroines who could overcome all obstacles and save the world.

As he got older, Hayao loved movies, especially animations. One day, a brave little girl in an animated film captivated him, and he decided to make his own stories.

After college, Hayao worked at an animation studio. He thought up and drew lots of exciting stories, and kids in Japan loved them.

However, not all of his animations were successful.
When one movie he had worked really hard on
became a flop, Hayao felt sad and disappointed.

But he knew he couldn't give up. He decided to try
something different—a cartoon series in his own
unique style.

This series grew into a beautiful movie about a brave girl named *Nausicaä* who tries to save her world, just as he had imagined for a long time.

Many people loved and praised it.

Because of its success, Hayao and his friends started their own place called *Studio Ghibli*, where they could make more movies the way they wanted.

At *Studio Ghibli*, Hayao created the famous movie, *My Neighbor Totoro*, about two sisters and a giant, friendly magical creature called Totoro.

This movie beautifully depicted friendship and the wonders of nature. To everyone's surprise, Totoro became a cultural icon, beloved by children and adults alike.

However, Hayao faced many challenges. Sometimes, his ideas were quite different from what other people expected.

Some people liked his work, but others thought it was too complicated or abstract for children. Regardless, Hayao kept pushing forward.

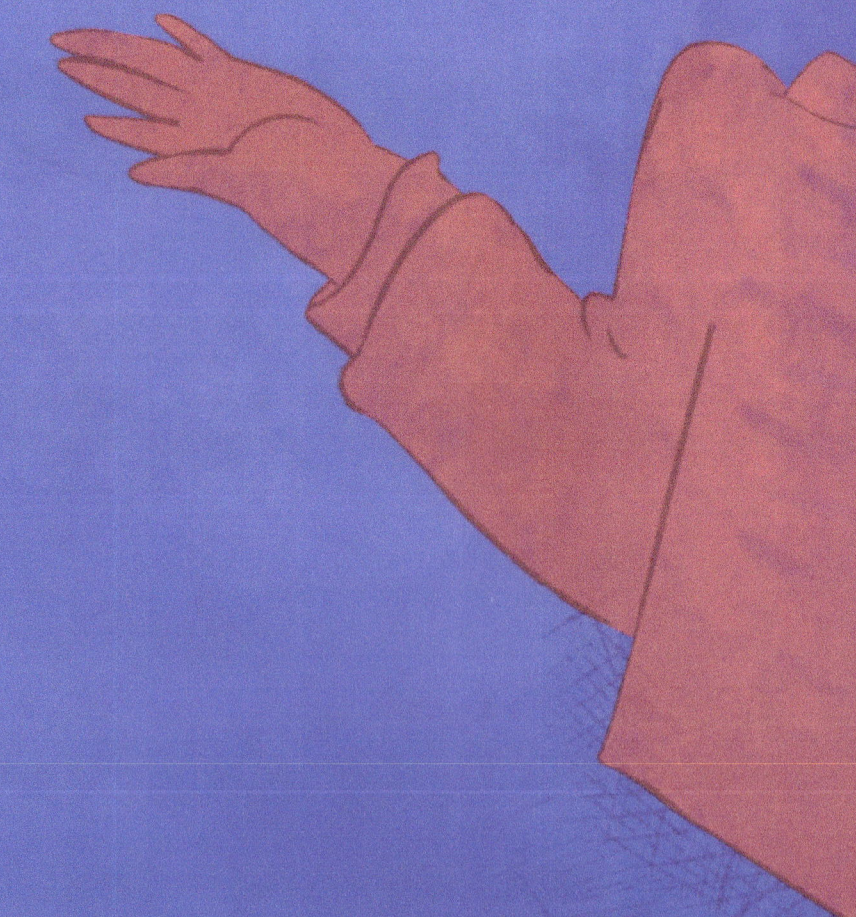

He surrounded himself with other talented artists and storytellers. They worked hard, supported each other, and focused on creating even more amazing stories that touched the hearts of many.

Each film Hayao and his friends made was filled with adventure and beautiful pictures.

His movies started winning renowned international awards and introduced global fans to the unique beauty of Japanese storytelling.

Hayao became famous all over the world. People eagerly welcomed him everywhere he went, excited to see his next creation.

But he always remembered his dreams as a little boy who loved to draw.

Hayao taught us that our imaginations can lead to great adventures. All we need to do is believe in our dreams, work hard, and never give up —just like the heroes in his movies.

Hayao Miyazaki's
Masterpieces

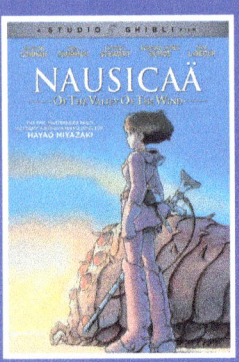

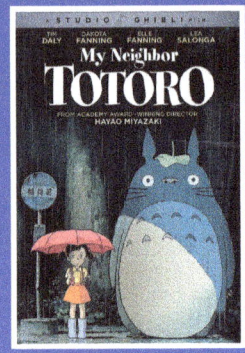

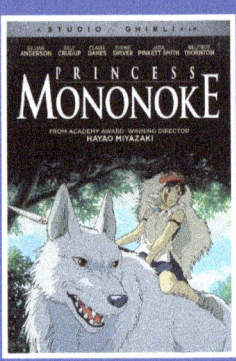

1984
Nausicaä of the Valley of the Wind

1988
My Neighbor Totoro

1997
Princess Mononoke

In many of Hayao Miyazaki's stories, the main characters are often girls. They are lovely but also bold and brave, ready to solve big problems. Hayao dreamed of a world where strong girls lead the way. Many people loved his idea of girl power, especially since it was unusual at the time.

My Neighbor Totoro was very popular in Japan and loved by animation fans around the world. But it was *Princess Mononoke* that made him famous everywhere.

2001

Spirited Away

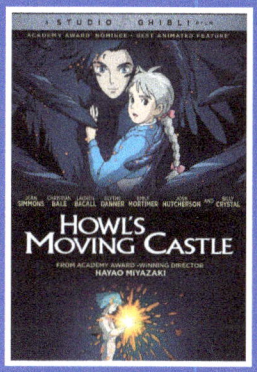

2004

Howl's Moving Castle

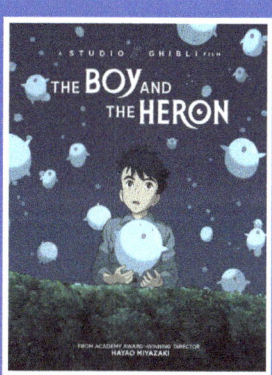

2023

**The Boy and
The Heron**

After that, *Spirited Away* came out, and people all over the world praised it as a wonderful masterpiece. This made more people discover his earlier movies, making *Studio Ghibli* and Miyazaki famous worldwide.

As he got older, he wanted to share his life stories and ideas with young people. So, at 82, he released his newest movie, *The Boy and The Heron*. This movie won him his first Golden Globe Award. His hard work and dedication made him a master of animation, inspiring many artists around the world.

UPFLY BOOKS

Photographic acknowledgements (pages 30-31): Amazon.com
All photos of movie posters (pages 30-31) © Studio Ghibli

Other Books by the Author

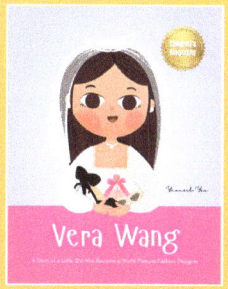

Hope you and your little one enjoyed our story!
If so, could you spare a moment to rate the book
or share your thoughts on Amazon?

Even a quick one-click rating would mean the
world to me. It helps me continue creating more
educational and fun stories for awesome kids like
yours.

Warm regards,
Yeonsil

P.S. Don't forget your free coloring + writing book:
upflybooks.com

www.ingramcontent.com/pod-product-compliance
Lightning Source LLC
Chambersburg PA
CBHW051629140626
46547CB00033B/2928